Chores

Nick Bruce

◇ ◇ ◇ ◇ ◇ ◇ ◇ ◇

broom

On **Monday** I sweep the floor.

box

On **Tuesday** I clean my room.

fork

spoon

knife

On **Wednesday** I set the table.

plant

On **Thursday** I water the plants.

trash

On **Friday** I empty the trash.

On **Saturday** my mom gives me
money for doing my chores.

money

I save the money in my money box.